# WHAT ARE

## rainbows made of?

## By Helen Orme

helping to explain
how the weather works

# WHAT ARE

## rainbows made of?

ticktock
MEDIA

Copyright © ticktock Entertainment Ltd 2003
First published in Great Britain in 2003 by ticktock Media Ltd.,
Unit 2, Orchard Business Centre, North Farm Road, Tunbridge Wells, Kent, TN2 3XF
We would like to thank: Lorna Cowan, Steven Dorling of the University of
East Anglia and Elizabeth Wiggans.
ISBN 1 86007 383 2 PB
ISBN 1 86007 389 1 HB
Printed in China
A CIP catalogue record for this book is available from the British Library.

# CONTENTS

Any words appearing in the text in bold,
**like this**, are explained in the Glossary.

Take a look out
of your window.
Weather is all
around us. What is the
weather like today?

A cloudy day

A sunny day

Heavy rain

Some days it is sunny when you wake up, but rainy after breakfast when you want to go outside to play. Sometimes the weather makes you feel hot and sometimes it makes you feel very cold.

But do you know what makes it **thunder**?

Or what rainbows are made of?

What makes our weather?

# How does the Sun make weather?

Lots of things make our weather the way it is, but the Sun is the most important.

The Sun is a giant ball of burning **gas**.

The Sun makes heat and light.
It warms up the **Earth** where we live, making perfect conditions for life.

Is the Sun smaller or bigger than our earth?
(answer on page 23)

Without the Sun we would not have sunshine!

The Sun heats up some parts of the Earth more than others.

North Pole, a cold place

The land and sea around the middle of the Earth at the **Equator** get hotter than the land and sea at the **Poles**.

Deserts are some of the hottest places on Earth.

Hottest places

The Equator

South Pole, a cold place

Antarctica (the South Pole) is one of the coldest places on Earth.

The warmer air and sea at the Equator moves from the hottest places towards the colder ones.

What are clouds made of?

a) Dust

b) Water

c) Snow

(You will find the answer on the next page.)

When this happens different types of weather are made.

# What are clouds made of?

**Clouds** look **solid**, but they are made up of millions of tiny drops of water and **ice crystals**.

These drops and crystals are so small that they float and move in the air.

Clouds with sharp edges are made of water droplets, while those with fuzzy edges are made of ice crystals.

Some clouds are low down on the ground. These clouds are called **fog.**

Weather changes all the time.
You might wake up in bright sunshine...

What are cirrus, cumulus, nimbus and stratus?

(answer on page 23)

...but after breakfast, the sunshine could be gone.

This is because clouds have covered the Sun.

It might even rain!

Why does it rain?

a) Because the air is too hot
b) Because the clouds are too heavy
c) Because the air is too cold

# Why does it rain?

**Clouds** bring rain. In the clouds tiny drops of water join together.

When the drops of water in a cloud get too big they are too heavy to stay in the air.

Then **raindrops** fall out of the clouds!

People wear special clothes when it rains so they don't get wet.

In some countries rain comes at special times of the year, called monsoon.

**Monsoon floods**

Where does all the rain go?
(answer on page 23)

Monsoon rain is very heavy and lasts for hours. Afterwards it will be very dry for the rest of the year.

Some places like this desert have very little rain at all.

How often does it rain where you live?

What are rainbows made of?

a) Water
b) Clouds
c) Coloured light

# What are rainbows made of?

Rainbows are made of coloured light.

Rainbows happen when the Sun comes out after it has been raining and there are still tiny water drops in the air.

The colours of a rainbow always appear in the same order – red, orange, yellow, green, blue, indigo and violet.

Sunlight shines through the **raindrops** and comes out as bands of coloured light. When this happens we see a rainbow.

Rainbow    Raindrop    Sunlight

It is impossible to reach the end of a rainbow.

What happens when you see two rainbows together?
(answer on page 23)

As you move, the rainbow you can see moves away at exactly the same speed.

Make your own rainbows by holding a **CD** out in sunlight. The shiny CD splits the **rays of light** in the same way a drop of water does.

What are hail and snow made of?

a) Ice crystals
b) Sunlight
c) Lightning

# What are hail and snow made of?

Ice crystals

Some rain begins as **ice crystals**. As they fall into warmer air most of these **frozen** drops **melt** into rain.

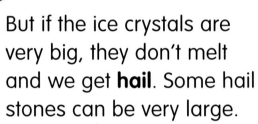

But if the ice crystals are very big, they don't melt and we get **hail**. Some hail stones can be very large.

In winter the air is often so cold that even smaller ice crystals won't melt.

How can snow cause sunburn?
(answer on page 23)

These small crystals stick together to make **snow**.

If the ground is as cold as the air the snow will **settle**.

Although every **snowflake** has six sides, no two snowflakes are alike.

Scarf

Gloves

Hat

If it snows for a long time the snow may get very deep. Time for some fun, but wrap-up warm!

What makes the wind blow?

a) Clouds moving

b) Moving air

c) Thunderstorms

# What makes the wind blow?

You can't see **wind** but you can see what it does.

It blows the leaves off the trees and makes their branches move around.

The wind even moves **clouds** along in the sky.

Wind happens when air moves from one place to another.

The wind can be very useful. **Windmills** have four long arms called sails that turn in the wind.

What do we use to measure wind direction? (answer on page 23)

The sails turn wheels inside the windmill. The wheels grind wheat into flour for making bread.

Today, we also build windfarms. The wind turns the sails of special windmills that can make electricity.

People in sports like windsurfing also use the power of the wind to ride along the waves.

## How strong can winds blow?

a) Strong enough to topple trees

b) Strong enough to wreck houses

c) Strong enough to make storms at sea

# How strong can winds blow?

Wind can be useful, but sometimes it is so strong it becomes frightening.

Trees sometimes lose their branches in autumn **gales**. But some winds do even more damage

**Hurricanes** are very, very bad wind storms. These storms begin out at sea, and they can travel great distances.

When they reach the land they do a lot of damage.

Hurricanes can blow cars into the air, rip the roofs off houses and pull trees out of the ground.

How fast can winds blow?
(answer on page 23)

**Tornadoes** are made of spinning wind. They look like funnels of dark **clouds** reaching up into the sky.

Tornadoes move very quickly across the ground. Like hurricanes, they wreck buildings.

What causes thunder and lightning?

a) Wind
b) Electricity
c) Fog

19

# What causes thunder and lightning?

**Thunderstorms** often happen in the summer when the air gets very hot.

Electricity is produced in thunderclouds.

We see this electricity as flashes of lightning.

When a thunderstorm happens at night the lightning is bright enough for you to see by.

If a **lightning bolt** hits something, it can cause a lot of damage. It strikes the highest object it finds. That can be a tree, a building or a person. Beware!

**A tree struck by lightning**

Lightning moves very quickly, heating up the air on the way. This causes **thunder**.

Why does lightning always come before thunder?

(answer on page 23)

Thunder is the loud noise that air makes when it has been made very hot, very quickly by the lightning.

Sometimes you get heavy rainfall...

...but some thunderstorms are dry. The **raindrops** dry up before they reach the ground.

# Glossary

**Bent** Turned and made to go another way.

**CD** A compact disc.

**Clouds** Masses of water drops floating in the sky.

**Earth** The planet we live on.

**Equator** An imaginary line round the middle of the Earth. It cuts the Earth into north and south. It is very hot at the Equator.

**Fog** Clouds on the ground that make it difficult to see.

**Frozen** A liquid (like water) that has got so cold it has gone solid and turned to ice.

**Gales** Strong winds.

**Gas** When some things are heated they turn into gas. Water turns into a gas called steam. The air we breathe is made from many gases.

**Hail** Small pieces of ice that fall to the ground.

**Hurricanes** Very strong winds.

**Ice crystals** Frozen raindrops.

**Lightning bolt** A single flash of electricity produced inside clouds. You see lightning bolts in the sky.

**Melt** When a solid turns into a liquid – usually because it has been heated. When ice is heated it melts and turns to water.

**Poles** The North and South

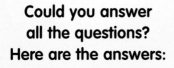

Poles are the places that are furthest away from the equator. It is very cold at the poles.

**Rays of light** Light that is moving in a straight line.

**Raindrops** Water from the clouds which falls as rain.

**Settle** Pile up on the ground.

**Snow** Lots of tiny falling ice crystals.

**Snowflake** A single flake of snow.

**Solid** Something that can be touched or held.

**Thunder** The sound made by lightning flashes.

**Thunderstorms** A storm where there is thunder and lightning.

**Tornadoes** Columns of spinning wind.

**Wind** Moving air.

**Windmills** Buildings with big sails that turn in the wind. The sails turn wheels that can be used to grind grain, or make electricity.

**Could you answer all the questions? Here are the answers:**

Page 6:  The Sun is much bigger than the Earth.

Page 9: Cirrus is a wispy cloud; cumulus a thick, fluffy cloud; nimbus a rain-bearing cloud; and stratus a cloud with lots of layers.

Page 11: Rain goes into rivers, the ground and down drains.

Page 13: When you see two rainbows together, the first rainbow has the colours the opposite way around to the second.

Page 14: Snow reflects sunlight very well, and can burn you.

Page 17: We use weather vanes – objects attached to the top of buildings that twirl round in the direction of the wind.

Page 19: In 1999, a tornado in Oklahoma, USA, reached speeds of up to 318 mph!

Page 21: Because light travels much faster than sound.

# Index

**t=top, b=bottom, c=centre, l=left, r=right,
OFC=outside front cover, OBC=outside back cover**

**Alamy images: 1cr & 4bl & 10bl & 22tl & 24tr, 2bl & 10br, 4tl & 8cl,
4tc & 16tl, 6tl, 8br, 9bl, 9tr, 11bl, 16bl, 16br, 18tl, 19t, 20t. Corbis: 2tl
& 15tr, 10tl, 18cl, 21cr. NASA: 4tr & 6cr.**
**Every effort has been made to trace the copyright holders and we
apologize in advance for any unintentional omissions. We would be
pleased to insert the appropriate acknowledgements in any
subsequent edition of this publication.**